Jack and the Beanstalk

Pantomime

Norman Robbins

Samuel French — London
New York – Toronto – Hollywood

For

MARTIN KINGSTON

The "simplest" Simon I've ever had the pleasure
of working with.

CHARACTERS

Jack Trot, a poor farmer's son
Dame Trot, his widowed mother
Simple Simon, her other son
King Hubert the Umpteenth of Serenia
Princess Melissa, his daughter
Rancid, the Ogre's Henchman
Fairy Thistledown, Guardian of Serenia
Giant Blunderbore
Daisy, the Cow
Adult Chorus of **Villagers, Gypsies, Slaves,** etc.
Junior and/or Babes chorus.

SYNOPSIS OF SCENES

ACT I

ACT II

AUTHOR'S NOTE

This version of *Jack and the Beanstalk* was written for the Queens Hall Theatre, Barnstaple, North Devon, and premièred there on 21st December, 1991 with myself as Dame Trot and the multi-talented Martin Kingston as Simple Simon. The show broke all box office records for pantomime at that venue, and this slightly modified version has now been made available for amateur societies. Unlike my previous pantomimes, I have not expanded the cast for amateur usage, as several groups have begged me for a small scale version of something. I trust this will meet with their approval. There *is* scope however for the experienced society to pad out the proceedings if they feel the need to do so.

Music should be bright and the pace of the pantomime kept brisk. Props have been kept to a minimum and apart from the "Black-Light" and strobe effects in the second Act, lighting should be no problem (even the smallest halls can cope with these nowadays). Our hysterical balloon ballet sequence in the Giant's kitchen scene may be impractical for some stages, but this can either be cut or be replaced by a "spot" such as a real ballet, conjuring act or performing seals (this is one of the few occasions in pantomime where a "spot" is acceptable as it is a *stated* "entertainment" within the plot line). The fierce sword fight between Rancid and Jack must be rehearsed most carefully. Don't leave this to the last minute. If an accident *can* happen—it *will*. Finally, I hope you derive as much fun from the show as we (and our audiences) did.

Norman Robbins 1992

Other plays by Norman Robbins published by Samuel French Ltd:

Aladdin
Ali Baba and the Forty Thieves
Cinderella
Dick Whittington
Grand Old Duke of York
Hickory Dickory Dock
Humpty Dumpty
Late Mrs Early
Nightmare
Pull the Other One
Puss in Boots
Rumpelstiltzkin
Sing a Song of Sixpence
Slaughterhouse
Sleeping Beauty
Tom, the Piper's Son
Tomb with a View
Wedding of the Year
Wonderful Story of Mother Goose

ACT I

Scene 1

A Village in Serenia

A typical pantomime village of half-timbered and thatched cottages with a background of green hills and trees. Entrances L *and* R *are concealed by shops or cottage fronts*

When the scene begins it is a sunny morning and the Villagers are singing and dancing on the Village Green, led by Jack Trot. He is a handsome youth dressed in clean, but well-worn clothes, and wears a ready smile

Song 1 (Jack and Villagers)

At the end of the song, Jack is C *with Villagers all around him*

Jack (*happily*) Ohhhhh, what a marvellous day it is. Not a cloud in the sky, or a care in the world. It's no wonder I keep bursting into song.
Girl Oh? We thought there was another reason entirely.

The Villagers agree with knowing looks and nods

Jack (*puzzled*) Like what?
Boy Like a certain Princess Melissa who comes an awfully long way each morning to collect the milk from your mother's dairy.
Girl And always needs help to carry it back to the palace.
Jack (*amused*) Oh, come on. You're not suggesting we're...? (*He laughs*) It's absolutely ridiculous. I mean—she's a princess and I'm just a poor farmer's son with a widowed mother to look after. She wouldn't give me a second glance.
Girl Perhaps not—but she did give you a kiss by the stile yesterday morning, didn't she?

All laugh good naturedly

Jack (*defeated*) Honestly, it's impossible to keep a secret in this village. All right. I admit it. We do love each other. (*Ruefully*) But unless I can find some way of making a fortune, there isn't a chance that the King will let us marry. (*He sighs deeply*) Oh, if only I could find a job.
Boy But you've already got one. You help your mother look after the dairy.
Jack (*scornfully*) Dairy. Just a tumbledown cottage and poor old Daisy

whose milk giving days are almost over. I'll never get rich selling milk. I want a well paid job. (*Ruefully*) The only trouble is, I've got no skills at all and everything I do is an absolute disaster.

Boy (*brightly*) Then why not apply to (*local District Council*)? They can always use another town planner.

The Villagers laugh

Jack (*brightening*) Well, I'm not going to worry about it today. For the next twenty-four hours I'm going to do nothing but enjoy myself.

Girl Is that so? (*She glances off* UL) Well here comes someone who may have other ideas about that—your mother.

Jack What? (*He turns and looks*) Oh, no. Quick, everyone. Out of sight. If she sees us standing here gossiping, she'll find jobs for all of us.

Jack and the Villagers exit rapidly in all directions. A moment later Dame Trot enters UL *with a shopping bag over her arm*

Dame (*calling*) Yoo-hoo. Are you there, Jack? I'm home. Yoo-hoo. (*She sees the audience and moves* DC *delightedly*) Ooh, I say. (*She beams at them fondly*) What a bonny looking lot. Oh, yes. Ever so up-market. Much better than the crowd we had last night. In fact there's one woman down here (*she indicates*) looks like a film star. Mind you, I've never been keen on horror films myself, but there you are. (*She grins*) Well, I'd better introduce meself, hadn't I? Trot's the name. Dame Trot of Trot's Lactic Emporium. (*To an audience member*) Don't look so worried, love. It's not an intellectual pantomime. We're very traditional in this part of the world. No ... A lactic emporium's just a posh name for a dairy. Well, you've got to sell yourself these days, haven't you? I mean, it's no use hiding your light under a bushel, whatever that means. You've got to advertise. Tell the world how good you are. It's the money, you see. There's not much about these days, is there? And the price of food. I've just been down to the shop for a bag of apples. Four pounds seventy. *Four pounds seventy*. For a tiny bag of apples. I only had a five pound note with me, so I had to give him that. I was just going out when he called after me: "Dame Trot—Dame Trot ... you've forgotten your thirty pence change." I said, "You'd better keep it, love. I trod on a grape on the way in." But it's the same everywhere, isn't it? They don't know what to charge you. And talk about rude. (*She grimaces*) Some of these shop assistants ... They look at you as though you were common as muck. (*She gives a look*) But they don't get the better of me. Oh, no. *I* look right back at 'em as though I'm *not*. Mind you, I went into a snack bar the other day for a bowl of soup and when it came, I took one look at it and sent for the manager. "I'm not eating this," I said. "It's not fit to serve to a pig." Ooh, he was ever so ajolopetic. "I'm so sorry, Madam," he said. "You shall have some that is." So you see, it pays to complain, doesn't it? Still, you don't want to listen to my problems, do you? I mean, we've all got 'em, haven't we, girls? Take the woman next door. (*She winces*) Talk about enjoying bad health. She's always at the doctors. I saw her in (*local chemist*) this morning, and there she was, moaning away about the medicine they'd just given her. "That's no use to me," she said. "It says on the bottle: 'For adults only' . . . and I've never had adults in me life." Mind you, it's about the only thing she hasn't had. The times she's been in hospital. Twenty-seven operations in the past three years to my knowledge. *Twenty-seven.* (*She winces*) They don't bother putting stitches in her now, you know. They've fitted her with a cat-flap. But it's her husband I feel sorry for. Oh, he does have some bad luck. He was up at the golf course last week and hit one ball so badly, it shot over a hedge and bashed a horse on the end of its nose. Well, the poor old horse bolted into a road, caused a car to swerve and smash into the side of a bus. The bus overturned, rolled down a slope on to a railway line and landed straight in front of an express train going eighty miles an hour. They ended up taking two hundred and fifty people to hospital. Well, the poor feller was distraught. "Whatever am I going to do?" he said. His partner looked him up and down and said, "It's your own stupid fault. How many times have I told you? For a shot like that, you should have used a number five iron." Still, no matter what goes wrong, you've got to keep smiling, haven't you? At least that's my motto.

Song 2 (Dame Trot)

The Villagers enter behind the Dame as she sings, joining in with singing or performing a dance routine. At end of the song, all exit cheerily

As they do so, the Lights dim

Rancid, the Giant's Henchman, enters UL. *He is a menacing figure, bearded, and carries a whip*

Rancid (*moving* DC, *sneering*) So this is Serenia, is it? Smug, self satisfied and wealthy Serenia. (*He laughs harshly*) There'll be rich pickings here for my mighty master. (*He glances around*) Now where shall I make a start?

Fairy Thistledown enters R

Fairy   One moment, friend. Your presence here is rather out of place.
       You enter fair Serenia with wicked heart and scowling face.
       Return at once to whence you came, or this I hereby swear,
       The might of fairy magic on your head I'll bring to bear.
Rancid (*glowering at her*) And who are you, might I ask?
Fairy   Why, Fairy Thistledown, of course. Defender of this land.
       To all who need protection here, I give my helping hand.
Rancid (*sneering*) How very noble of you. (*Harshly*) But take my advice and keep your long nose out of things that don't concern you. I am Rancid, Henchman to Blunderbore the Giant, and here in this village to do his

bidding. From this day on, Serenia belongs to him and all who live here must give up their wealth or die. (*He laughs harshly*)

Fairy (*scornfully*) I fear he's much mistaken if that's really his intention.
He'll find that I will scotch his plan, by subtle
     intervention...
So if my warning you ignore, you'll very quickly see
That all his schemes will come to grief, and *that* I
     guarantee.

Rancid (*amused*) I can't tell you how frightened we are. (*He laughs harshly then snarls*) Lift one finger to stop me doing his will, and we'll see who comes off best. My master will grind your bones to make his bread.

Fairy (*unconcerned*) So be it, then. The die is cast. A battle you propose.
From henceforth on, without a doubt, we'll be the deadliest of foes.
I'll put a stop to Blunderbore—of that you may be certain.
And on his wicked life let down the very final curtain.

Fairy Thistledown exits R

Rancid (*gazing after her*) Threaten away, you simpering sprite, but Serenia *still* belongs to Blunderbore and no-one shall wrest it from him. (*To the audience*) But now to continue with my task: the collection of every penny this miserable Kingdom possesses.

Rancid laughs harshly and exits L

The Lights return to normal

Simple Simon enters UR. *He is a cheery individual in patched, but clean clothing in bright colours. He moves* DC

Simon (*brightly*) Hiya, kids. (*He gives a huge smile*)

Audience reaction. His smile fades

(*Peering out into the audience*) Is anybody there? (*Calling again*) Hiya, kids.

Audience reaction

Ohhhhh, come on. You can do better than that, can't you? I get more noise pouring milk on me Rice Krispies. (*Realizing*) Oh, of course. You don't know who I am, do you? I've not introduced myself. (*He slaps his left shoulder*) Oooh, I am a fool. (*Firmly*) My name is... (*he hesitates*) er ... er... (*He looks worried then brightens*) Oh, yes. My name is *Simple Simon*. (*He grins*) I thought I'd forgotten, for a minute. Yes. My name is Simple Simon, and I live down at the dairy with me mum and our Jack. Have you met him—our Jack? He's ever so nice, isn't he? Mind you—(*he glances around to see no-one is listening*) he's a bit peculiar. (*He nods*)

I mean, how many fellers do you know who walk about wearing lipstick, false eyelashes, high heels and fishnet tights? But I shouldn't make fun of him, should I? 'Cos he's ever so good to me. Ever since we were little he's shared everything he had with me. Mumps, measles—chicken pox. We even shared nappies when we were babies. Well, me mum was so poor it was the only way she could make ends meet. Anyway, I expect you're all wondering why they call me *Simple* Simon, aren't you? Well, it's not because I'm daft, you know. I once did a fifty piece jigsaw puzzle in only six months—and that's not bad, is it? It said, "Five to seven years" on the box. No, the reason they call me Simple Simon is because I've got a terrible memory. I can't remember things. I even forget my own name. Well, you noticed that, didn't you? (*He thinks*) Here, hold on, though. You can help me remember that, can't you? 'Cos every time I come on, I'll shout "Hiya, Kids", and you can shout back, "Hiya, Simon". Will you do that for me? Will you? All right then, we'll have a little practice.

He rehearses with the audience until satisfied

That's smashing. Right, well I'll have to get going now, 'cos I've got to give Daisy the Cow a wash and brush up, but I'll see you all later. And don't forget—(*shouting*) hiya, kids.

Simple Simon exits DR

There is a fanfare

The Villagers quickly enter, and the Town Cryer enters UL

Cryer (*grandly*) His Royal Majesty, King Hubert the Umpteenth of Serenia, and his daughter, the Princess Melissa.

All cheer

King Hubert enters UL *followed by Princess Melissa. They move* DC

King (*pleased*) Oh, I say. How nice. I never realized I was so popular. (*He gives a short chuckle; to Melissa*) Off you go, dear. Pay the royal milk bill and try not to be too long. We mustn't be late for the market.
Princess (*quickly*) Oh, you don't have to wait for me, Father. I can make my own way there.
King Nonsense, m'dear. Can't have you walking round the countryside on your own. Besides, I can have a look round while I'm waiting. It's been years since I visited this part of Serenia.
Princess Really?
King Oh, yes. But I've never forgotten it. You can get the most wonderful bargains here, you know. I bought a burglar proof safe for only fifty pounds, and three days later, there it was wide open and everything I'd put inside it had gone. (*He beams happily*)

Princess (*puzzled*) What's wonderful about that? I thought you said it was burglar proof.

King Well wasn't that proof we'd had a burglar?

The Crowd look amused

Oh, and there's a lovely little restaurant just down the road. I remember going there for lunch one day. Seven home-made sausages I eated. (*He licks his lips at the memory*)

Princess (*smiling*) No, no, Father. You mean *ate*.

King (*surprised*) Do I? Well, maybe you're right. I know I eated a lot.

The Crowd laugh

Anyway, off you go, dear, and I'll see you when you get back.

The Princess shakes her head in despair and exits DR *with a smile*

Now what shall I look at first? (*He ponders*)

Girl Why not visit the amusement arcade, Your Majesty?

King Amusement arcade? Why on earth should I visit an awful place like that? They're a complete waste of good money.

Boy Perhaps so, Your Majesty. But where else can we go these days? There isn't a theatre for miles, and television hasn't been invented yet. We've got to have somewhere to entertain ourselves.

King But you don't need amusement arcades for that. Why, when I was a boy, when *we* wanted to entertain ourselves, we just dressed up in our Sunday clothes and went for a walk.

Girl That doesn't sound very exciting to me.

Others agree

King Maybe not. But it certainly does the trick.

Song 3 (King and Villagers)

At the end of the song, all exit happily. As they do so, Rancid enters DL, *an almost empty pouch in his hand and a scowl on his face*

Rancid (*hefting the bag*) Bah. Only five pounds collected. The people here are poorer than I thought. This will never satisfy my master, the Giant. He'll be so annoyed, he might eat me. (*He tucks the bag in his belt*) I've got to find money quickly. But where?

The Dame enters R, *singing happily*

Dame (*singing*) Put on your Sunday clothes when you feel down and out... (*She sees him*) Oooh, I say—it's (*well-known unpopular figure*).

Rancid (*scowling*) Bah. Who are you?

Dame Titania Trot, Seductress of Serenia and widow of this parish. (*She flutters her lashes at him*)

Rancid Indeed? (*With menace*) And do you know who I am?

Dame (*wide-eyed*) Why? You've not lost your memory, have you? (*Concerned*) Oh, you poor thing.

Rancid (*loudly*) I am Rancid, Henchman to the Giant Blunderbore—New ruler of this miserable kingdom.

Dame (*impressed*) Oooh, I say.

Rancid Now hand over your money, or suffer my master's anger.

Dame (*amused*) Hand over me money? You must be joking. I'm so poor I have to take the bones out of me corsets to make soup with.

Rancid (*annoyed*) Ten thousand curses. Have no rich people been born in this revolting little place?

Dame No. Only babies.

Rancid (*snarling*) Very well, then. As you refuse to pay, my master will have no choice but to bring ruin to the entire country.

Dame Don't be daft. The (*ruling political party*) are doing that already. (*Soothingly*) Look, there's no need to get all nasty. If you're so short of money I'll tell you what to do. Get your pen-knife out, find a nice piece of wood, whittle it down into strips then take 'em along to the (*local bank*) and have a word with the manager.

Rancid (*curious*) And how will that help me get money?

Dame (*to the audience*) You're going to love this. (*To Rancid*) You tell him you want to open a shavings account.

As Rancid reacts, she chortles with laughter and pushes him playfully, sending him flying

(*To the audience*) Ooooh, I've been saving that one up for ages. (*She chortles*)

Rancid (*glowering*) So, you like a little joke, do you? Then let's see you laugh this off. Unless you find one hundred pounds for me by tomorrow morning, (*moving behind her*) I'll have you skinned alive, boiled in oil and sliced into little—tiny—pieces. (*He chuckles nastily and moves* DR)

Dame (*startled*) A hundred pounds? Where am I going to get that sort of money from? There isn't a hundred pounds in the whole village.

Rancid (*smirking*) Then you'd better make the most of your last day on earth, hadn't you?

Rancid exits DR, *giving a harsh laugh*

Dame (*stricken*) Oooh, I say. Whatever am I going to do?

Simon enters UR

Simon (*to the audience*) Hiya, kids.

Audience reaction

Hiya, Mum. I've cleaned the cow-shed out and I've... (*He notices she is upset*) I've—I've... Is something wrong?

Dame (*worried*) Oh, Simon. Some nasty old giant's henchman's just been here and told me if I don't hand over a hundred pounds by tomorrow morning, he's going to have me boiled in oil.

Simon Oo-er.

Dame (*sniffling*) And I was so looking forward to me twenty-fifth birthday.

Simon Don't worry, Mum. We'll find the money somehow. (*Suddenly*) Here, how about having a collection from the audience? I bet they've got plenty of money. (*To the audience*) Anybody out there got a few fivers to spare?

Dame (*pushing him*) Behave yourself. You can't ask them for money. They need it for coffee and ice cream in the interval. No, we've got to find it ourselves. (*Worried*) But where are we going to look? (*She remembers*) Here, wait a minute. We've still got Daisy, haven't we? Maybe she can help us? If she's got any milk left we can sell it at the market this afternoon. Tell everybody it's the same milk the king drinks, and they'll pay a fortune for it.

Simon Oh, we can't do that, Mum. Our Jack——

Dame Never mind our Jack. Stop arguing and give her a shout. Where is she?

Simon I don't know... But if I ask all my friends in the audience to give her a shout, maybe she'll hear it and come running. (*To the audience*) Will you do that for us, everybody? Will you?

Audience reaction

Altogether then, after three. One, two, three... (*Calling*) Daisy.

To the strains of "Daisy Bell", Daisy the Cow dances on UR *and frisks about happily*

Dame (*to her*) All right. All right. Settle down. Settle down.

Daisy calms down and the Dame leads her DC

Now then, Daisy. How about doing a little curtsy for all the boys and girls in the audience? Just to say thank you for shouting so loud. Would you like to do that?

Daisy nods

I thought you would. Go on then.

Daisy curtsies to the audience

(*Fondly*) There. (*To the audience*) And would you like to say hello to Daisy, boys and girls?

Audience response

All right, then. Altogether. One, two, three...

Audience response

(*To Daisy*) You see? They like you, don't they?

Daisy nods

Now then, Daisy. We're in a bit of trouble, so we're going to need a drop more milk. (*To Simon*) Aren't we, Simon? (*To Daisy*) Can you do that for us?

Daisy shakes her head

(*Surprised*) No? Of course you can. (*To Simon*) Go get a bucket and stool and make a start.

Simon (*surprised*) Me? You want me to do it?

Dame Of course I want you to do it. We're having salad for lunch so I've got to go and cut the privet. Now get on with it and stop wasting time.

Simon (*protesting*) But I can't milk a cow. I'm daft, I am. I don't know anything about 'em.

Dame Then it's about time you learned. There's nothing to it, is there, Daisy?

Daisy shakes her head

You see? Look. I'll tell you what I'll do. I'll ask you a few simple questions about her and we'll see how much you do know about cows. And Daisy'll help you, (*to Daisy*) won't you, Daisy?

Daisy lets out a loud "Moo"

Now then. What did that sound tell you about this cow?

Simon She does smashing impressions of (*popular female rock singer*).

Dame (*glowering at him*) Now without looking at her—tell me what she looks like.

Simon (*closing his eyes*) She's got one head—one tail—and five legs.

Dame (*startled*) Five legs?

Simon (*opening his eyes*) Yes. (*Pointing*) One, two, three, four—and there's the udder. (*He chortles*)

Dame (*dazed*) I think I'd better ask you something simpler. Name me something that comes out of cows?

Simon Simple. The Isle of Wight Ferry.

Dame (*angry*) No, it doesn't. Milk comes out of cows. (*Spelling*) M—I—(*she hesitates*)—ilk.

Simon Not from this cow it doesn't.

Dame Oh yes it does.

Simon Oh no it doesn't.

Audience participation

Dame Well we'll see about that. Get the bucket and stool and I'll prove it to you.

Simon exits R

Daisy turns sideways to the audience, facing L

Simon enters with a bucket and stool

Simon (*looking at Daisy*) Here, that cow's giving me funny looks.
Dame Don't be daft. You were born with those. Now put the bucket under there ... (*She moves to the front of Daisy*)

Simon goes behind Daisy, places the bucket under her udders and moves to tail end of her

(*To Daisy*) Now then, Daisy. I want two gallons in that bucket, please. Off you go.

Daisy shakes her head

I said I want two gallons of milk, please.

Daisy shakes her head again

(*Annoyed*) Ooooooh, you naughty, naughty, naughty cow.
Simon No, she isn't. I've been trying to tell you. Our Jack's already milked her and she hasn't got two gallons left.
Dame Well why didn't you say so before? (*To Daisy*) I'm ever so sorry, love. How much have you got left?

Daisy whispers in her ear

You've only got tinned milk? Well, give me some tinned milk then.

Daisy wriggles and a large tin of milk falls into the bucket. Simon picks it up

Simon Here, it's empty. (*He reads the label*) Oh, no wonder. It's evaporated milk. (*He laughs and tosses the tin off stage*)
Dame (*annoyed*) Ooooooooh, you naughty, naughty, naughty cow. (*To Simon*) We're going to have to do this by hand. Put the stool down, sit on it, grab the dangly bits and ring dem bells.

She moves behind Daisy to the rear of the cow. Simon sits on the stool with his back to the audience, raises his arms and flexes his fingers. As he does so, Daisy moves forward and beyond him. The Dame glances round

Not there, you fathead. The bucket goes under her. (*She rolls her eyes*)

Simon gets up, repositions the stool and bucket, sits—and Daisy moves forward again. Simon, not noticing, grabs at nothing and falls flat on his face

(*Irritated*) What are you doing down there?
Simon (*weakly*) Getting up. (*He staggers to his feet*)
Dame Put the stool over there (*She indicates the original position*) and I'll move her back to you.

Simon moves the stool back L and sits. The Dame pushes Daisy back towards him

Simon (*calling*) Left a bit ... right a bit ... left hand down ... this way ...

Daisy sits on Simon's lap

Oooh, gerroff.

He pushes Daisy off him and jumps to his feet

Dame (*to Daisy*) Oooh, you are being a bad girl this morning. We're never going to get any milk at this rate. (*To Simon*) Get out of the way and I'll show you how it's done. (*She turns aside and thinks*) Now what do I do first?
Simon (*helpfully*) Sit on the stool.
Dame (*remembering*) That's right. Sit on the stool.

Daisy sits on the stool and crosses her legs

(*To her*) Not you, fathead. Me. Get up.

Daisy shakes her head

Dame } (*together*) Oooooh, you naughty, naughty, naughty cow.
Simon }
Dame We'd better lift her off.
Simon Good idea.

They try to move behind her, but Daisy revolves on the stool to remain facing them

Dame (*throwing up her hands, defeated and moving front*) I give up.
Simon No, wait. I've got an idea. (*He hurries to her*)

Simon is about to tell Dame when he realizes that Daisy is listening intently. He pulls Dame DR and begins to whisper. Daisy gets up and tiptoes down to above and behind them to listen. They finally turn to see the empty stool and bucket

Dame (*startled*) She's gone.
Simon Quick. Let's get rid of these before she comes back.

They hurry to the stool and bucket, Daisy following behind unnoticed

The Dame takes the stool off L *and returns*

Simon tosses the bucket off R

There is a loud cry from the King who comes staggering on with it over his head

The Dame and Simon react

King (*reeling about*) Help. Help.

They hurry over and remove the bucket. The King's crown is missing

(*Weakly*) Quick. Quick. Call out the guards.
Simon (*worried*) Oooh, there's no need for that, Mr King. It was only an accident. (*To the audience*) Wasn't it, kids?

Audience reaction

King (*annoyed*) Do as I say. This means jail.
Dame Oo-er. And I've already been a prisoner in Cell Block H.
King (*testily*) What are you talking about?
Dame I once hit my husband with a sponge cake and went to jail for five years.
King Don't be ridiculous, woman. You don't get jailed five years for common assault.
Simon No. But she told the judge she'd baked it herself—so he altered the charge to assault with a deadly weapon.
King (*irritated*) Oooh. (*Loudly*) Help. Help.

Jack, the Princess and Villagers enter

Princess (*anxiously*) What is it, Father? What's wrong?
King (*wailing*) I've been robbed.

Everyone reacts with shock

Simon (*protesting*) I only hit him with the bucket.
King No, no. I've been robbed by a man named Rancid—henchman to the Giant, Blunderbore. He's stolen the royal crown.

All react with dismay

Jack Don't worry, Your Majesty. He won't get far. The guards are sure to catch him.

King How can they? He'll be miles away by now. (*He groans*) What am I going to do? I'm opening the Great Market in half an hour and I can't appear without a crown.

Princess Perhaps (*local jeweller*) can make you one?

King And how would I pay for it? The villain took all my money, too. (*Suddenly brightening*) Wait a minute. Of course. I'll collect all the rent money people owe me. That should cover it nicely.

Dame (*horrified*) Oh, no. I haven't paid mine for ten years.

King (*ignoring her*) Off you go, everybody. Bring your rent monies at once. And if anyone doesn't pay up, I'm going to be very, very, cross indeed. (*To the Princess*) Come along, Melissa. We'd better see the jeweller right away.

The King exits L

Princess (*to Jack; hastily*) I'll see you later, Jack.

The Princess follows the King off. The Villagers disperse concernedly

Simon That's torn it. Where are *we* going to get money from?

Jack (*helplessly*) We'll just have to sell something.

Dame (*brokenly*) But what? We've got nothing left to sell.

Jack (*reluctantly*) Nothing—except Daisy.

Simon Oh, no.

All look at Daisy in dismay, as she hangs her head in sorrow. The Lights slowly fade to a Black-out and the scene ends quietly

SCENE 2

On the way to market

A lane scene depicting trees, fields and distant buildings. If this is not possible, it may be played in front of a plain cloth

The Fairy enters R

Fairy Although for poor Serenia it seems that trouble's brewing;
Old Blunderbore shall *not* triumph. Jack Trot shall see to his undoing.
And though vile Rancid may attempt to put him to the test,
With *me* to guide him, Master Jack, I vow, will come off best.

She smiles and exits R. *As she does so, Jack enters* L, *holding a short tether which is fastened around Daisy's neck. Both Jack and Daisy look most unhappy*

Jack Come along, Daisy. Only another mile to go before we reach the Market.

Daisy pulls back

Oh, I know you don't want to be sold, but there's nothing else we can do. The King wants his rent money and if we don't sell you, we'll be in real trouble.

Daisy whispers in his ear

What? (*He hugs her tightly*) Of course I won't sell you to anybody called McDonald or Wimpy. (*Trying to be cheerful*) Maybe I can find somebody rich to buy you? Someone who'll love you just as much as we do and who'll give you a nice warm shed—lots of sweet grass and fresh, fresh clover ... and if I can do *that*, why, everything will be fine, won't it?

Daisy begins to nod, but changes the movement to a sad shake of her head

(*Sighing*) You're right. It won't be anything of the kind. (*With sudden determination*) But it won't be forever, I promise you. As soon as I've made my fortune, I'll buy you back again and we'll all live happily ever after. (*Dejectedly*) The only trouble is, I haven't the faintest idea of how I'm going to do it.

The Princess hurries on L

(*Surprised*) Melissa. What are you doing here?
Princess I've just heard the news about Daisy. Oh, Jack. You can't possibly sell her at the market.
Jack (*helplessly*) What else can we do? She's all we've got left in the world.
Princess Then why not let us buy her?
Jack You mean ... you and the King?
Princess Why not? We'd give you a good price for her.
Jack But what would you do with her? You couldn't keep a cow at the palace.
Princess Of course we couldn't. But we could ask you and your mother to look after her for us, couldn't we? That way, you wouldn't be losing her at all.
Jack (*eagerly*) Do you really mean that? (*Relieved*) Oh, Melissa—it'd be the perfect solution. (*Anxiously*) But would your father agree?
Princess There's only one way to find out and that's to ask him. The market's just down the road, so if you bring Daisy along, he can give you an answer right away. Besides, (*demurely*) it'll give us a chance to spend a little more time together.
Jack (*happily*) Oh, if only I could be sure this isn't a dream.
Princess (*amused*) Whatever do you mean?
Jack Only a few minutes ago, I was the saddest man in all Serenia, but now everything's looking up again—and it's all thanks to you. Oh, Melissa ... You're the best thing that's ever happened to me. However could I live without you?

Princess That's something I hope you never find out.

Song 4 (Jack and Princess)

At the end of the song, they exit R, *leading Daisy*

The Lights fade to a Black-out and the end of the scene

SCENE 3

The Great Market

A great country market with tents, stalls, cattle-pens, etc., and trees to mask entrances. Full lighting

When the scene begins, solemn-faced Citizens of Serenia, are standing around watching a band of Gypsy Dancers dance a wild Hora, tambourines jangling furiously

Dance (Gypsies)

At the end of the dance, the Gypsies give a triumphant cry and strike a pose. Everyone applauds and the Gypsies quickly unfreeze to brandish their tambourines for monetary reward. The Citizens sadly shake their heads and show their empty pockets and purses before moving off. The furious Gypsies glower after them and shake their fists in disgust before exiting. King Hubert enters UL *wearing a badly made, tatty-looking cardboard crown with gold paper stuck on it*

King (*groaning*) Oh, it's hopeless. Hopeless. The market's teeming with people, but no-one's got anything to spend. That nasty Giant's Henchman has robbed them all. (*He takes off his crown*) And look at this. An old cornflake box with toffee papers and beads stuck on it. Was ever a king as poor as I am?

The Fairy enters DR

Fairy Fear not, most gracious Majesty. A champion's at hand.
And very soon prosperity will cloak again this pleasant land.
Though Blunderbore—and Rancid—may *appear* to hold the aces . . .
A humble farmer's son will shortly put *both* in their rightful places.
King (*gaping at her*) W—what? Who are you?
Fairy The Guardian of Serenia. My task? To ease your plight.
All wicked schemes to overthrow. All wrongs to put to right.
And this I promise faithfully; your crown I shall restore . . .
Tomorrow night shall see the end of mighty Giant Blunderbore.

The Fairy exits

King (*startled*) But—but ... Wait. (*He blinks*) She's gone. (*He shakes his head to clear it*) I must have been seeing things. There's no such thing as fairies. (*Weakly*) Ooooh, I've gone all of a tiz-was. I'll have to lie down for a minute. (*He begins to stagger* L)

The Princess enters R, *followed by Jack and Daisy*

Princess (*hurrying to him*) So there you are, Father. We've been looking all over for you.

King (*turning to her*) Oh, Melissa. Thank goodness you've arrived. We've got to go home. Immediately. (*He clutches at his head*)

Princess Home? But we've only just got here. And besides, there's something I want to ask you.

King (*weakly*) Eh?

Princess You know how fond you are of the milk we get from Dame Trot's Dairy? Well, Jack, here, is selling the cow, so I thought we might like to buy her.

King (*brokenly*) Buy her? With what? There's hardly a penny left in the country. I can't afford to change my mind, now, let alone buy a cow.

Jack (*anxiously*) But she's the best milker in all Serenia, Sire.

Daisy nods

King Perhaps she is—but unless we get our money back from that terrible Rancid character, nobody will be able to buy her. We're all ruined. Ruined.

The Princess and Jack react

Jack In that case, Your Majesty, there's only one thing to do. Find out where he's hiding himself and teach him a lesson he'll never forget.

King (*worried*) And risk upsetting the Giant? (*He shakes his head*) Oh, no. We couldn't do that. He'd trample us into the ground. (*He shudders*)

Jack (*protesting*) But you can't let him get away with robbing everyone.

King (*despairingly*) What else can we do? No-one can fight a Giant. (*He sighs deeply*) Come along, Melissa. We'd better be on our way. (*He moves* L *dejectedly*)

Princess (*to Jack, quickly*) Don't worry, Jack. I'm sure we'll think of something.

The Princess hurries after the King and they both exit L

Jack (*looking after them*) No-one can fight a giant, eh? (*Grimly*) If I had a good sharp sword, I'd face an army of giants. (*Downcast*) But swords cost money—and that's another thing I haven't got. (*To Daisy*) Come on, old girl. We'd better have another walk around the market. (*He sighs deeply*) Oh, if only I could sell you. I'd buy myself the finest sword in all Serenia and show Blunderbore and his henchman exactly where to get off.

Jack exits UR *followed by Daisy. As they go, Rancid enters* DL, *scowling*

Rancid (*harshly*) Oh, you would, would you? Then I'd better make sure you never get the chance.

Rancid exits. Dame Trot enters DR

Dame Oh, I say. Isn't this exciting? The biggest market there's been for years. Have you seen all the people? (*She chuckles*) Our Jack shouldn't have any trouble selling Daisy here, should he? Then once we've got some cash, I can pay the king his rent money, give old Rancid his hundred pounds, and there might be a little bit left over for spending. (*Seriously*) Mind you, I shan't be spending it on anything daft. Oh, no. Not like the woman next door to us. She bought a parrot here three years ago. A great big green parrot. The feller said, "You can't go wrong with this, missis. It'll repeat every word it hears." Well, she was over the moon with it. Took it all over the place, showing off and waiting for it to say something. But it never did. Not a sausage. She kept it two years then brought it back. "Here," she said to the feller, "I bought this parrot two years ago, and you told me it'd repeat everything it heard." "That's right," said the feller. "It will." "Well how is it," she said, "it hasn't opened its mouth in two years? Is it poorly or something?" "Course it's not poorly," he said. "It's deaf." (*Knowingly*) Ohhh. You've got to watch 'em, haven't you? I mean, you don't know who you're dealing with these days, do you? Only last week, I went out shopping and missed the bus home. I was ever so upset because it was nearly milking time and I had to get back for that, didn't I? So I looked around and there outside the (*local hotel*) was this feller—medals all over his chest and covered with gold braid. I thought, "The very man", so I went over to him and I said, "Excuse me, Doorman, but would you mind calling me a taxi to take me home." He said, "How *dare* you, Madam? I'm not a doorman. I'm an Admiral in the Royal Navy." I said, "In that case call me a boat. I'm in a hurry." (*She shakes her head*) But you wouldn't believe the trouble I had in ... (*She stops*)

Simon enters R

Simon (*to the audience*) Hiya, kids.
Dame Never mind "Hiya, kids". What are you doing here? I told you to stay at home in case anybody called, didn't I?
Simon Yes, I know. And somebody did. This smashing looking blonde came round collecting for a swimming pool. (*He drools with delight*)
Dame (*worried*) Oh, no. You didn't give her anything, did you?
Simon (*nodding*) Yes. A bucket of water. (*He chortles*)
Dame (*reacting*) Oooooh, you're as daft as your dad was, you are. Thank goodness you're not an inventor as well.
Simon (*surprised*) Eh? I didn't know me dad was an inventor.
Dame Well of course he was. That's how he got killed, isn't it? Testing his latest invention—the Irish parachute.
Simon Irish parachute?
Dame Yes. It opened on impact. (*She sniffs back a sob*) And look at the

state he left me in. A poor young widow with two sons to look after, and nothing but a run-down dairy with only one cow left to milk. (*She sniffles*) And we haven't even got her, now. (*She sobs*)

Simon (*soothingly*) Cheer up, Mum. Things'll get better.

Dame Well they can't get any worse, can they? (*She mops her eyes*) Go find our Jack and see if he's managed to sell Daisy yet. It's time I was getting back to the village, anyway. I've got to practice me shouting and screaming for this afternoon.

Simon (*puzzled*) Shouting and screaming?

Dame (*nodding*) I'm playing tennis with (*famous tennis player*) so I've got to be able to make a lot of noise, haven't I?

Simon What for? You don't make a noise playing tennis.

Dame Of course you do, stupid. Whoever heard of anyone playing tennis without raising a racket?

Simon is speechless

She exits R

Simon (*to the audience*) And people call *me* Simple.

The Babes enter excitedly

Babes Simon. Simon. (*They cluster around him*)

Simon Oooh, it's the children from the village. What are you so excited about?

Babe 1 (*amused*) We've just seen the funniest bull in the cattle market. It's only a baby and it's as white as snow.

The Babes giggle

Simon (*reprovingly*) Here, you mustn't laugh. It could be a very special bull, that could.

Babe 2 (*scornfully*) How could a white bull be special?

Simon Quite easily. And if you'll listen carefully, I'll *tell* you.

Song 5 (Simon and Babes)

At the end of the song, Simon and Babes exit DR. *A moment later, Jack despondently enters* UL *with Daisy*

Jack (*moving down* C) It's no use, Daisy. We've been all round the market and no-one wants to buy you. Looks like there's nothing left to do but make our way home again.

Rancid enters L, *disguised in a hooded cloak and stooping like an old man*

Rancid (*in quavery tones*) Young man. Young man.

Jack turns to see him

That's a fine looking cow you have there. She wouldn't be for sale by any chance, would she?

Jack (*brightening*) Why, yes. She is. But I want a good price for her—at least five gold pieces.

Daisy nods

Rancid Five gold pieces? (*He chuckles*) A cow like this is worth a bagful of gold pieces.

He produces a small, well-filled bag from beneath his cloak and holds it up. Jack gapes in surprise

See. (*He hands the bag to Jack*)

Jack quickly opens the bag and peers inside

Jack (*awed*) I don't believe it. I've never seen so much gold in my whole life.

Rancid (*taking the bag back*) Then the cow is mine?

Jack (*after a slight hesitation*) Providing you promise to take good care of her.

Rancid (*leering*) Oh, I'll take care of her all right..

Jack Then it's a deal.

Rancid Good. (*He turns aside and quickly changes the bag of gold for a similar looking one*) There's the gold. (*He gives it to Jack*) And the cow is mine. (*He snatches the rope from Jack's hand in triumph*)

Jack (*looking at the bag in delight*) I can't wait to tell Mother the news. (*To Daisy*) Goodbye, Daisy. Be a good girl. (*He gives her a quick hug around the neck*)

Jack exits R

Rancid (*throwing back the hood and straightening*) The gullible fool. (*He laughs harshly*) Wait till he finds out what's really inside that bag. Nothing but a handful of worthless beans. (*He laughs again then tugs nastily on Daisy's tether*) And as for you, you scraggy-looking bag of bones—I'll have you made into a pie for the giant's dinner.

He turns to exit but Daisy refuses to move. Furious, he turns back

So. Try to defy me, would you? Well let's see how you like this. (*He produces his whip and raises it to strike Daisy who cowers*)

The Princess enters DL hurriedly

Princess (*calling*) Jack. Jack. I've had an idea ... (*She stops in her tracks as she sees Rancid with Daisy*) Oh.

Rancid (*turning to her*) By the great eye teeth of Blunderbore. The most beautiful creature I've seen since I arrived in Serenia. My master would reward me well if I returned to Giantland with her. (*Quickly grabbing her wrist*) Come along, my pretty one. There's someone who'd like to meet you.

Princess (*startled*) How dare you? Let go of me. (*She struggles*)

Rancid (*amused*) Struggle away, my dear—but your struggles will be in vain. From now on you belong to Blunderbore the Giant—to do with as he wishes. (*He laughs harshly*)

Princess (*calling*) Help. Help.

Grabbing Daisy's rope again, Rancid tugs on it harshly

Rancid Now come. To the Castle in the Clouds.

Laughing harshly, he drags the struggling Princess and the reluctant Daisy off DL

The Lights fade rapidly to a Black-out

SCENE 4

On the way home

A lane scene. As Scene 2. Full lighting

The Fairy enters R

Fairy As homeward bound he hurries down this winding, earthen track,
The time has come for fairy spells to aid our hero, Master Jack.

She waves her wand gracefully

Upon that bag of worthless beans, enchantment now is placed.
And though, for just a little while, 'twill seem he's been disgraced,
Those magic seeds will carry him to fame and fortune vast—
And mighty Giant Blunderbore will meet his match at last.

The Fairy exits. Jack enters L, *with the bag of beans*

Jack I still can't believe it. A whole bag of gold pieces. Just wait till Mum sees it. She'll be so excited.

Simon enters R

Simon (*to the audience*) Hiya, kids. (*To Jack*) Here—where's Daisy? You haven't really sold her, have you?

Jack (*delightedly*) I certainly have. For a whole bag of gold. Look. (*He displays the bag*)

Simon (*impressed*) Oooh, hey. We're rich.

Jack I'll say we are. There's enough money here to pay off all our debts and buy me a sword.

Simon (*blankly*) What do you want a sword for?

Jack To fight the Giant with, of course. I'll teach him not to attack honest citizens and steal their money. By the time I've finished with him, he'll wish he'd never heard of Serenia.

Simon (*wide-eyed*) Here, what's got into you? You've never said boo to a goose before.

Jack I know. But from now on things are going to be different. There's something to fight for, and I'm just the man to do it.

Song 6 (Jack)

Jack and Simon exit at the end of the song. Rapid fade to Black-out

Scene 5

Dame Trot's dairy

Full or three-quarter set. A dairy interior. If possible, a half-open window should be set in the backcloth. Full lighting inside, but darkening out

When the scene begins, Milkmaids and Farmhands are performing a lively dance

Dance (Chorus)

At the end of the dance, Dame Trot enters L *and is surprised to see them*

Dame What's going on? What do you think you're playing at? Dancing round me dairy at this time o' night. Go on. Out. The lot of you. Shoo. Shoo. (*She ushers them off*)

The Chorus exit in good humour

(*To the audience*) I wouldn't mind so much, but there's nothing for 'em to do here now Daisy's gone. (*She sniffles and dabs at her eyes*) Poor Daisy. I'm missing her already. (*She blinks back tears*) I've had that cow ever since she was an Oxo cube. (*She sniffles*) She was just like one of the family. (*She gives a sudden glare into the audience*) Who said: "Yes—and I know which one"? (*Worried*) Oh, but I wish our Jack'd hurry up and get back from the market. Look at the time. He should have been here ages ago. I hope nothing's happened to him.

The King enters

King Aha... Dame Trot. Just the woman I'm looking for.

The Dame preens herself

I've called to collect the rent money you owe me. (*Hopefully*) You do have it, don't you?

Dame (*taken aback*) Well, not at the minute, dear. I'm still waiting for our Jack to get back from the market.

King (*crossly*) Oooh, don't mention the market to me. I've a good mind to have it closed down. They're nothing but a bunch of crooks and swindlers.

Dame (*startled*) Eh?

King I bought a set of Snow Tyres for the royal coach this afternoon, and by the time I got home, they'd all melted.

Dame (*shocked*) Oh, I say. Still, never mind, dear. Let's go into the kitchen and I'll make you a nice cup of tea while we're waiting. I'd offer you a slice of cake as well, but it came out of the oven like a lump of lead. (*She grimaces*) Oooh, I wish I knew how to make me cakes light.

King You could always try soaking 'em in petrol.

They both laugh uproariously

Dame (*mopping at her eyes*) Ooh, I haven't laughed so much since you took me out in your electric car twenty years ago.

King (*fondly*) Ah, yes—my famous electric car. (*He frowns*) But what was funny about that?

Dame Well, we only got to the bottom of the drive, didn't we?

King I know. But the cable wouldn't stretch any further. Still, I never bother with cars these days. Whenever I've a free moment, I go out on my favourite gee-gee, (*names a famous Derby or National winner*).

Dame (*impressed*) Oh, I say.

King You get a much better view from the back of a horse, you know.

Dame I suppose so, but if it's views you're looking for, why don't you ride on top of a double-decker bus?

King Don't be silly. I'd never get the horse up the stairs. (*He beams*) Oh, it is nice to see you again, Titania. I'm sorry about all that fuss this morning, but being robbed by that nasty giant's henchman made me quite forget my manners. You will forgive me, won't you?

Dame (*coyly*) Oh, think nothing of it.

King (*relieved*) Ah, you're still as sweet as ever. I can't understand how we ever came to lose touch. Why on earth didn't you come to the palace and visit us?

Dame Well, we never had the time. Me and old Trotty had only been married a year when we heard the patter of tiny footsteps.

King (*beaming again*) Oh, yes. The children.

Dame No. The mice. They were all over the place. That's why we're so poor. They ate everything we had. (*She sniffles*) And now he's gone as well and I haven't a penny left in the whole wide world.

King (*glumly*) Me neither. And as soon as the servants find out I can't pay their wages, they'll be off like a shot. It's going to be so lonely without them.

Dame (*brightening*) Oh, well, there's no need to be lonely. (*Coyly*) Haven't you ever thought about having your nuptials spliced again?

King (*startled*) I beg your pardon?

Dame Well, you're a widower—and *I'm* a widow. Why don't we blight our troth and get joined together in holy bedlock?

King You mean—you want me marry you?

Dame Why not? Then I could be Queen of Serenia and have me features stamped on a coin. (*She simpers and preens*)

King (*aside*) They look as though they've been stamped on already—by an elephant. (*To her*) I'm sorry, Titania, but it's quite out of the question. We're far too old for all that.

Dame (*vamping him*) Don't you believe it, Hubert. You're never too old to fall in love.

Song 7 (Dame and King)

At the end of the song, the Dame lunges at the King who gives a yell of fright and dashes off R. *The Dame follows in a flurry of skirts. As they exit, Jack and Simon enter* L, *excitedly*

Simon (*to the audience*) Hiya, kids.

Jack (*looking round*) Mother. Mother. Where are you?

Simon (*calling*) Mum.

Jack (*happily*) Oh, just wait till she sees this. (*He displays the bag again*) She'll be the happiest woman in all Serenia.

Simon Here, she might even take us down to the (*local entertainment centre*) to celebrate. There's a fabulous new entertainer on there tonight. He does farmyard impressions.

Jack What's fabulous about that? Anybody can make animal sounds.

Simon Oh, he doesn't do the sounds. He does the smells.

The Dame enters excitedly

Dame Oh, thank goodness you're back. Quick. Quick. How much did you get for poor Daisy?

Jack Look. (*He holds up the bag*)

Dame (*gaping*) Oh. We're rich. Rich. (*She grabs the bag excitedly*) Now we'll be able to pay off all our debts and have enough left over to buy one of those great big houses like they have in (*local district*). All bay windows and split-level floors.

Simon Don't be daft, Mum. They haven't got split-level floors. That's subsidence.

Dame (*fumbling with the bag*) Oooh, I'm all fingers and thumbs. (*She opens it and looks inside*) Ohhhhhhh. (*Her jaw drops*)

Jack (*frowning*) Is something wrong? Aren't you pleased?

Dame Pleased? *Pleased?* That you've sold our only cow for a bag of mouldy old beans?

Jack
Simon } (*together*) *Beans?*

Dame (*stricken*) They haven't even got tomato sauce on them.

Jack (*worried*) You must be mistaken.

Dame (*sharply*) Don't you tell me I'm mistaken. I can recognize tomato sauce when I see it. (*Wailing*) Oh, whatever are we going to do?

Jack (*helplessly*) But—but it's supposed to be gold.

Dame (*angrily*) Gold? If you think this is gold, then you're even more stupid than he is.

The Dame indicates Simon who reacts

Jack (*dazedly*) I don't understand.

Dame But I do. I understand I've got a worthless son who's sold our only possession for a bag of beans that are no good for anything but this. (*She crosses to the window and hurls the bag out. Brokenly*) Now get to bed, the pair of you. The bailiffs'll be here in the morning to throw us into the street.

Sobbing bitterly she totters off R. Jack and Simon look at each other in disbelief, then move slowly off L. Simon exits and Jack hesitates to gaze at the window before following

The Lights fade to a Black-out

The Fairy enters in a follow spot

Fairy   In the garden, by the gate,
     The magic seeds now germinate.
     Swiftly rooting, shoots a-curling,
     Tendrils clinging, leaves unfurling,
     Sprouting, branching, twisting, quick'ning,
     Growing faster, strength'ning, thick'ning.
     Past the roof—the old church spire—
     Soaring upwards, ever higher,
     Reaching for the Land of Cloud
     Where Blunderbore, that Giant proud
     Imagines from all harm he's free...
     But come the morn—we'll see. We'll see.

The Fairy exits

The Lights brighten full, revealing the fact that the dairy has vanished and we are now in the garden

SCENE 6

Outside the dairy

UR *can be seen the rear of dairy. A picket fence extends from this, right across the stage to vanish off* L. *Behind the fence,* UC, *is the beanstalk, its top lost to sight, and its base surrounded by light mist*

Children enter L, *playing a game. They see the beanstalk, react, then scurry off again quickly with much excitement*

The Villagers enter sleepily, pulled by the Children and they too react at the sight of it

Villagers (*variously*) What is it? Where did it come from? (*Etc.*)

Simon enters in his nightgown, clutching a stuffed toy

Simon (*to the audience*) Hiya, kids. (*Seeing the beanstalk*) Ooooh. What a big stick of rhubarb.

The Dame enters in her nightgown, followed by Jack, who is dressed

Dame What's all the noise about? (*Seeing the beanstalk*) Aghhhhhh.
Jack (*awed*) It's a giant beanstalk. It must have grown from the beans you threw out of the window last night. (*He gazes upwards*)

The King enters DL *in a fluster*

King Help, somebody. Help.

Everyone turns to him

It's Melissa. My beautiful daughter. She's been kidnapped by the Giant and his henchman.

All react with dismay

My Lord Chamberlain saw it all. A huge arm came out of the clouds and carried her off, together with everything that's been stolen. (*In despair*) Oh, what am I going to do? I can't even send my army to rescue her.
Jack (*stepping forward bravely*) But there's nothing to stop me going.
Simon How can you? There's no way up there. (*He indicates upwards*)
Jack You think not? (*He points to the beanstalk*) Well what about that. By the look of things, it goes straight up to Cloudland, and if I climb to the top, you can bet your life it'll lead me right to the giant's castle.
Dame (*worried*) But you can't go up there. Not on your own. And besides— you know you can't stand heights. You get dizzy if you stand on a thick carpet.

King (*eagerly*) Rescue my daughter and I'll give you anything you want.
Jack Don't worry, Your Majesty. She'll be back in Serenia before the day
   is out—and with any luck, I'll deal with old Blunderbore, too.

The Villagers cheer loudly

Song 8 (Jack and Company)

*At the end of the song, Jack begins to climb the beanstalk and the first Act
ends with everyone waving and cheering him on his way*

*If possible, after the Curtain falls, it can rise again on a tableau depicting Jack
several feet above the heads of the others as——*

—*the* CURTAIN *falls*

ACT II

At the top of the beanstalk

The backdrop depicts rolling countryside. Entrances and exits are concealed by trees

When the CURTAIN *rises, Fairies are dancing to a slow, dreamy melody*

Ballet (Fairies)

At the end of the dance, they strike an attitude as Fairy Thistledown enters and moves DC

Fairy   Here, halfway twixt earth and sky,
        The youth you all admire,
        Has almost reached; yet o'er his head
        The magic beanstalk grows still higher.
        Soaring up to where on
        Drifting clouds so soft and pliant,
        Is built great Castle Thunderstorm—
        The home of Blunderbore, the Giant.
        To this strange place, young Jack ascends
        On valiant quest intending,
        And so our fairy aid we'll give
        And lead him on to happy ending.
        Come, brave champion from below,
        We greet you with delight—
        And fame and fortune shall be yours
        I vow, this very night.

She waves her wand and all exit in a flurry. A moment later, Jack enters R

Jack (*wiping his brow*) Phew. That beanstalk's even higher than I thought it was. It's no wonder my arms ache so much. I've been climbing for hours. (*He looks around*) So this is Cloudland? I'd never have dreamed somewhere like this was floating about over my head. But where's the giant's castle? If only I knew which way to go. (*He yawns*) Oh, and I'm so tired. Perhaps I'd better have a rest before I go any further. I want to be wide awake when I meet up with old Blunderbore. (*He picks a resting place* UL) This looks fairly comfortable. (*He settles himself down*) Just a few minutes sleep, then I'll be on my way again. (*He yawns, stretches and falls asleep*)

The Fairy enters

Fairy   Enfolded deep in magic sleep
                               Our youthful hero now doth rest;
                               Awak'ning in a little while
                               To find himself in armour dress'd.
                               Yet whilst he sleeps, sweet gentle dreams
                               His mind will occupy,
                               And creatures of great beauty
                               Fill the vastness of the sky.

She waves her hand and the Lights fade rapidly to a Black-out

The Fairy and Jack exit in the darkness

UV lighting is switched on and the Fairy sings on an off-stage mic.

Song 9 (Fairy)

Butterflies, etc., enter during the song and move around in character

Just before the end of the routine, Jack enters in a silver costume and resumes his original sleeping position. The Butterflies, etc., exit

UV lighting is switched off

The Fairy enters in a follow spot to sing the last few lines of the song. The Fairy exits at the end of the song

The Lights return to normal. Jack awakens

Jack (*stretching*) Ohhhh, I feel a lot better for that. (*Noticing his change of clothing*) What? (*Astounded*) What's happened to me? These clothes... (*He looks around*) Am I dreaming? Perhaps I'd better pinch myself to make sure. (*He does so*) Owwww. Well, I'm certainly not dreaming—but I don't understand. Where on earth did they come from? (*He examines himself again*) They're quite a good fit—and comfortable, too. But all the same... (*He looks round again*) Well, I suppose I'll have to keep them. There's not a sign of my own clothes, anywhere. This place is even stranger than it looks. Still, if this is the worst thing that's going to happen to me, I've nothing much to worry about. But now to find the giant's castle and rescue Melissa.

Jack exits DL. *As he does so, Simon enters* R *dressed as a Cub Scout*

Simon Hiya, kids. Dib dib dib. Dob dob dob. A-ke-la. (*He salutes*)

The Dame enters in a Brownie outfit

Dame Never mind dib dib dib. Where's our Jack got to? He can't be too far in front.

Simon Oh, don't worry, Mum. He can look after himself.

Dame (*tartly*) That's what you think. I'm not having a son of mine wandering round foreign places all on his ownsome. You never know what might happen to him. That's why we've followed him up here. To make sure he doesn't get into trouble.

Simon (*glancing around*) Here, you don't think it might be dangerous, do you?

Dame Of course it might be dangerous. There's a man-eating giant rambling round the place, isn't there? But you needn't worry. If he lays one finger on my little Jack, he'll find out he's got me to reckon with.

Simon (*surprised*) You?

Dame Yes. I haven't told anybody up to now, but I've got a black belt in karaoke. (*Airily*) Course, it runs in the family, you know. All your aunties and uncles were experts at something. Your Uncle Fred, for instance. He was the strongest man in the world.

Simon Gerraway.

Dame (*insistent*) He was. I remember once, they locked him in a little iron cage, tied it up with thick steel chains, fastened them with a burglar proof padlock and threw away the key. Then they bet him a hundred pounds he couldn't get out again.

Simon (*interested*) And what happened?

Dame He squeezed one arm through the bars, wrapped it round the chains and got a firm grip on the padlock. Then he took a big breath, flexed his muscles and twisted. Like this. (*She demonstrates*) And before anybody could blink, he'd broken it in six places. (*She looks smug*)

Simon (*awed*) Broken the padlock?

Dame No. His arm. Had it in plaster for weeks, poor love.

The King enters L painfully

King (*groaning*) Oooooh.

Dame (*surprised*) Hubert. What are you doing here?

King (*testily*) What do you think I'm doing? I'm following you. (*He groans*) Oooh, my poor feet.

Dame What's the matter with 'em?

King It's these shoes. They're three sizes too small. (*He groans*)

Simon Well why don't you get a pair that's the right size?

King Why should I? My kingdom's bankrupt. My crown's been stolen and my poor little daughter's been kidnapped by a giant. Taking these shoes off is the only bit of pleasure I've got left. (*He winces in pain*)

The Villagers enter L, looking around

Simon Oooh, look. It's all the people from the village. What are they doing here?

King They came with me. We're all so worried, you see.

Dame Worried? (*Amused*) There's nothing to be worried about. It's all going to turn out fine.

King How do you know?

Dame I watched all the rehearsals.

Simon Mum's right. There's nothing to worry about. And even if there was, we'd know just what to do about it.

King Really?

Dame Yes. Just listen, and we'll tell you.

Song 10 and Dance (Dame and Simon)

As they sing, the King and Villagers join in a lively tap-dance. At the end of the routine, the Giant's voice is heard. All react in fear

Giant (*off*)   Fee, fi, fo, fum.
                    I smell the blood of Englishmen.
                    Be they alive or be they dead ...
                    I'll grind their bones to make my bread.

Everyone screams in terror and they exit in all directions

The Lights rapidly fade to a Black-out

SCENE 2

On the way to the Giant's castle

A lanecloth depicting a rocky pass and stunted trees

The Princess hurries on L, *in some distress*

Princess (*calling*) Help. Help. (*She looks round for somewhere to hide*)

Rancid enters L, *smirking*

Rancid It's no use trying to escape, my dear. There's no way down to earth unless the giant himself lowers you. (*He chuckles*) Now why not be sensible and return to the castle?

Princess (*defiantly*) Never.

Rancid (*snarling*) Stupid girl. He's taken quite a fancy to you. Be nice to him and you won't find things too bad. Annoy him, and he'll grind your bones to make his bread.

Princess I don't care. I'll never be nice to that horrible monster. I hate him.

Rancid (*shrugging*) Very well, then. If you won't come back to the castle,
 · stay where you are. I've far more important things to do than chase you around Cloudland. The giant wants cow pie for supper, and there's a

certain bag of bones in the meadow that'll do just nicely for that. (*He laughs harshly*)

Rancid exits L

Princess (*horrified*) Oh, no. Poor Daisy. Baked inside a pie for the giant to eat. I've got to save her. But how? (*She thinks*) Perhaps if I go back to the castle, I can persuade him to eat something else? I don't want to, but it's the only thing I can think of. (*Calling*) Mr Rancid. Mr Rancid—wait.

The Princess hurries off after him. As she vanishes from sight, Jack hurries on R

Jack (*eagerly*) Melissa? Melissa? (*His shoulders slump in disappointment*) I thought I heard her voice—but it must have been wishful thinking. (*He moves* C *with a sigh*) Oh, if only I knew she was all right. And where's the giant's castle? I hope I haven't come all this way for nothing.

The Fairy enters R. *She carries a sword*

Fairy One moment. Ere you stray inside old Blunderbore's domain,
You'll need protection, otherwise no victory you'll gain.
Take this. A magic sword. Its blade the sharpest ever known.

She hands the sword to him

Used well, its power will aid you, and the Giant *shall* be overthrown.

The Fairy exits swiftly

Jack Wait. (*He hurries after her then stops*) She's gone. (*He looks at the sword*) A magic sword, eh? Well if it is, then it's just what I need to teach old Blunderbore a lesson. (*He executes a few swift movements with it*) Right, Mr Giant. You've had things your own way for far too long. Now if Lady Luck's with me, it's time to start fighting back.

Song 11 (Jack)

At the end of the song, Jack exits L

The Lights fade rapidly to a Black-out

SCENE 3

In sight of Castle Thunderstorm

A full set. The backdrop depicts a thick forest of sinister-looking trees which

almost form an arch to frame the fearful-looking castle built upon a distant mountain-top UC. *Gigantic Venus fly-traps and other evil-looking plants, mask entrances and exits*

Rancid enters R, *a sword in his belt, pulling the reluctant Daisy behind him*

Rancid (*snarling*) Hurry up, you flea-bitten old bonebag. The giant wants his supper and you're it. (*He laughs harshly*) You'll go down a treat with a ton of potatoes and some nice fresh vegetables.

Daisy shivers in fright

(*In mock concern*) Ahhhhh. A little bit cold, are you? Never mind. You'll soon warm up with a nice blanket of pastry over you. (*He laughs harshly*)

Simon enters R, *singing cheerily*

Simon "She'll be coming round the mountain when she comes. She'll be coming round the mountain when she comes." (*He notices the audience*) Hiya, kids.
Rancid (*astounded*) You. How did you get here?
Simon Never mind about how I got here. What are you doing with this cross-eyed, knock-kneed, bow-legged, bony old broken-down gorilla?
Rancid *Gorilla?* That's a cow, you fathead.
Simon I wasn't talking to you.
Rancid (*annoyed*) Aaaaagh. I'll tear you into little pieces, you miserable moron.
Simon Here, who are you calling a moron? I went to Oxford University, I did.
Rancid (*taken aback*) Really? And what did you study?
Simon Nothing. It was shut. (*He chortles*)

Rancid reacts

But I know everything there is to know about history.
Rancid (*sneering*) Oh, you do, do you? Then tell me this. Who was the first woman in the world?
Simon Easy, it was ... er ... er ... er ... Just a minute. (*He thinks*)
Rancid (*amused*) I'll give you a clue. She had something to do with an apple.
Simon (*remembering*) Oh, yes. Granny Smith.
Rancid (*drawing his sword and advancing on Simon*) Do you know what I'm going to do with this?
Simon Toast a crumpet?
Rancid (*fiercely*) I'm going to carve you into little pieces, and turn you into a cow pie with her. (*He indicates Daisy*)
Simon (*backing away*) Ooo-er. (*Wailing*) Mother. Help. (*He cowers*)

As Rancid advances on Simon, Daisy suddenly scrapes her hoof and charges him from behind, jabbing him in the rear with her horns. With a howl of pain,

Rancid turns to face her as she lowers her head for a second charge

Rancid (*scared*) Aaaagh. (*Retreating*) Back. Back.

Daisy charges again. Rancid turns quickly and runs in a circular route with Daisy in hot pursuit

The terrified Rancid exits L

Daisy does a victory dance

Simon (*to the audience*) Three cheers for Daisy, kids. Hip, hip...

Audience reaction. Daisy curtsies, etc.

Jack enters R, *sword at the ready*

Jack What's all the noise about? (*Seeing them*) Simon. Daisy. What are you doing here?
Simon I followed you up the beanstalk—and it's a good job I did. That nasty old Rancid was going to turn Daisy into a cow pie.

Daisy nods

Jack (*astounded*) What?
Simon Yes. But Daisy fixed him, (*to Daisy*) didn't you, Daisy?

Daisy nods and attempts to look modest

Jack Well done, old girl. But we'd better not hang around here. We could all be in terrible danger. This is the Land of Giants, and that over there (*indicating*) is the Castle of old Blunderbore.

A series of heavy, descending chords are played by the orchestra

Simon (*nervously*) What was that?
Jack What was what?
Simon That "da, da, da, da, daaaaah" when you said, "The Castle of Old Blunderbore".

The chords are played again and Simon looks around him in a startled manner

Jack (*shrugging*) I didn't hear anything. Perhaps it was an echo?
Simon Oooh, I've heard about echoes. I knew a feller from (*local district*) who absolutely loved 'em. Went all over the country looking for the best ones. Then one day he found a big cave—ever so dark, it was—and he stood right outside the entrance and shouted "Yoo-hoo". And a few seconds later, this sound came back at him, ever so faint. "Yoo-hoo."

Oh, he was tickled pink. He couldn't wait to try it again. So he filled his lungs as much as he could, shouted "Yoo-hoo" at the top of his voice and ran into the cave to hear it better.

Jack And did he?

Simon No. He got run over by the four-thirty train from (*local city*).

Jack (*amused*) Well, that's all very interesting, but we haven't time to stand here talking. I've got to get to the giant's castle and rescue Melissa.

Simon You mean we have. Me and Daisy are coming with you. Aren't we, Daisy?

Daisy nods firmly

Jack All right, then. But we've got to be very, very, careful.

They exit L, cautiously. As they do so, Dame Trot enters R in yet another dreadful creation

Dame (*excitedly*) Oh, I say, boys and girls. You'll never guess what. Old Hubert's just proposed to me and we're going to get married. (*She simpers*) Oooh, I can hardly believe it. I've always wanted to be a queen. (*Suddenly gives a dirty look to the audience, then continues*) Hey, just think. No more getting up at half-past four in the morning to milk the cow. From now on, I'm going to be waited on hand and foot. (*She chortles, then sobers quickly*) Mind you, I never thought it would happen. Well, you don't, do you, girls? I mean, it's not often you get a second chance when you've lost your first. Of course, some are luckier than others, aren't they? I read in the paper last week that one of them Hollywood film stars had just cremated her tenth husband. It's always the way, isn't it? Some girls can't get a man at all, while others have husbands to burn.

The King enters R, clutching his nose

King (*groaning*) Ooooh. Oooooh. (*He stumbles to her*)

Dame (*startled*) Hubert. Whatever's the matter, dear?

King I was sniffing a wild brose over there—(*he indicates*)—and I got stung. Oooooh.

Dame (*blankly*) A wild *brose*?

King Yes. Yes. B.R.O.S.E. Brose.

Dame (*realizing*) No, no, no, no, no. You mean a wild *rose*. There's no B in rose.

King There was in the one I sniffed. Ooooooh.

Dame (*quickly*) Here ... let me put some ointment on it.

King Don't be silly. It'll be miles away by now. (*Seeing the castle*) Oh. Look. It's the Giant's castle.

Dame (*looking*) Oh, I say, isn't it creepy? It looks just like (*local derelict site, or government block*)

King (*bravely*) Don't worry, Titania. I'll look after you.

Dame (*pleased*) Will you?

King Of course I will. After all, we're going to be married, aren't we?

Dame (*remembering*) Oh, yes. (*Suddenly*) Hey, but there is one thing. You won't be going off and leaving me all the time like my first husband did, will you?

King (*surprised*) Leaving you?

Dame Oh, yes. He was always off looking for excitement and adventure. You know how some fellers want to go all around the world in a rowing boat? (*She shakes her head*) Not my husband. He wanted to cross the Atlantic on a plank of wood. England to America.

King And did he do it?

Dame Course not. He couldn't find a plank long enough.

King Well, you needn't worry. I won't be leaving you. (*Passionately*) Oh, Titania, give me one little kiss from those ruby red lips.

Dame (*coyly*) Ooooh, I don't know that I should. After all, I've never kissed a man before. (*She simpers*)

King Neither have I, so don't let that stop you.

Dame (*delightedly*) Oh, you sauce-pot.

Song 12 (King and Dame)

At the end of the song, they exit

Rapid fade to Black-out

Scene 4

Outside the Giant's castle

A lane scene. The backdrop depicts the castle walls and a few gnarled trees. The scene is dreary and lit in greens and blues

The Princess enters L, *looking dejected. She moves* C *as the Giant's voice is heard*

Giant (*off*) Fee, fi, fo, fum.
　　　　　Bring me food to fill my tum.
　　　　　(*Calling*) Rancid. Rancid. Where are you, you snivelling wretch? Raaaaaancid.

The Princess cowers and covers her ears

Princess Dreadful monster. He wouldn't even listen to me when I begged him to spare poor Daisy. (*Despairingly*) Oh, what am I going to do?

Jack enters R

Jack (*seeing her*) Melissa.

Princess (*delightedly*) Jack.

They hurry to each other

Oh, thank goodness you've found me. But how did you get here?

Jack I'll tell you later. But first I've got a little score to settle with old Blunderbore. (*He displays the sword*)

Princess (*quickly*) No. It's much too dangerous. A sword can't hurt him. He's taller than a house and has the strength of a hundred men.

Jack Don't worry. This is no ordinary sword. One jab and it'll be all over for Mr Giant.

Princess (*concerned*) But what if something goes wrong and he kills you? I couldn't bear to stay here for the rest of my life. It's so dark and gloomy.

Jack Nothing will go wrong. I promise. As long as I know you love me, I'll face a thousand giants and beat them all. So cheer up. From now on, we're going to live happily ever after. (*He sheaths the sword*)

Song 13 (Jack and Princess)

At the end of the song, Princess glances off R *and gives a cry of alarm*

Two armed Guards enter with drawn swords

Jack quickly turns to face them and draws his own sword while Melissa backs away L

Rancid enters L, *sword at the ready, and grabs her*

As she cries out in surprise, Jack turns back to her and sees Rancid

Rancid (*harshly*) One move and the girl dies.

He signals to the Guards who relieve Jack of his sword and menace him

(*Smirking*) And what have we here, then? Another puny earthling eager to meet the King of Giants. (*With great menace*) And so you shall, my friend. So you shall.

Rancid laughs harshly and with Melissa still in his grasp, exits L. *Jack follows, urged by the swords of the two Guards. As they all exit, King Hubert's head appears* R *to watch them go. A moment later, he enters in distress*

King Oh, dear. (*He tiptoes* L, *still watching them*) Now what are we going to do? I'd better go for help.

The King begins backing cautiously R

Simon enters R, *backing cautiously* L

They collide and react with cries of fright

(*Turning*) Simon.

Simon Your Magneticals. (*He sighs with relief*) Oooh, you didn't half give me a fright. (*To the audience*) Hiya, kids.

King (*anguished*) Shhhhhhhh. Shhhhhhhh.

Simon (*looking round*) Here, where's me mum? You haven't lost her, have you?

King No, no. Of course not. She's quite safe. I left her a few miles down the road. She said she couldn't walk another step.

Simon (*worried*) Here, I hope she's all right.

The Dame enters R *in another gown*

Dame Of course I am, dear. I know how to look after meself. Sorry I'm late, but I had a bit of an accident on the way here. I borrowed a BMX mountain bike, and I was just coming down (*local street*) when I got a puncture in me front tyre.

King Oh. Ran over a nail, did you?

Dame No, no. It was a bottle of whisky.

Simon Bottle of whisky? Couldn't you have steered round it?

Dame How could I? I didn't even see it. The stupid woman had it in her shopping bag. (*She beams*) Anyway, why are you standing out here?

King That nasty old Rancid's just caught your Jack trying to rescue my darling Melissa. He's taken them in to see the giant.

Simon Ooo-er. What are we going to do?

Dame We'll have to think of a plan to rescue them. (*She glances around*) But we won't do it here, eh? I don't like the look of it. I think it might be haunted.

King (*airily*) Oh, don't worry about that, Titania. If it is haunted, we can always keep the ghosts away by singing a little song. They don't like music, you know.

Dame (*impressed*) Don't they?

Simon Course they don't. It frightens them to death.

The Dame pushes him

Dame Well, all right then. Let's think of something to sing.

King How about "She's only a surgeon's daughter, but she certainly knows how to operate"?

Simon No, no. There's too many verses in that. How about (*selected song*)?

Dame Oooh, yes. We all know that one. Here, there's just one thing, though. What if while we're singing this beautiful old madrigal, something nasty and horrible creeps up behind us?

King Don't be silly, Titania. There are no politicians in tonight.

Simon No. But Mum's right. We don't want taking by surprise, do we? I know. I'll ask all my friends in the audience to help us. (*To the audience*) If anything nasty creeps up behind us, will you shout out and warn us? Will you?

Audience reaction

Oh, smashing. (*To the others*) See. I told you they would. We can start
singing now.

They begin to sing

After a few bars, a Ghost enters L *and drifts off* R

The audience reacts and the singers stop and look puzzled

Simon (*to the audience*) What's wrong? What is it?

Ad-lib with the audience, then the singers continue again

The Ghost enters R, *crosses* L *and exits*

*Audience reaction stops the singers. Again there is general ad-lib until they
decide to have a look round. All tiptoe* R *and take a circular route*

The Ghost enters L, *tagging on behind them and exits* R

The others resume their original positions

Dame (*disgustedly*) Oh, there's nothing there at all. They're pulling our legs.
Let's carry on singing.

The singing begins again

The Ghost enters and hovers behind them

Audience reaction stops the singing

Simon (*to the audience*) What's the matter now?

General ad-lib with the audience

King (*scared*) Behind us? There's a ghost *behind* us?
Dame I'll tell you what we'll do. We'll count three, then turn round quickly
and grab it. All right? One, two——

The Ghost bobs down

——three.

The trio turn quickly and fail to see the Ghost. They turn back in disgust

King (*annoyed*) That's done it. We're not going to waste any more time.

They can shout as much as they like now, and we're not going to take any notice.

Simon Right. Let's carry on singing.

They begin to sing again. The Ghost rises and taps the King on the shoulder

The King turns and sees it and runs off L, followed by the Ghost

Simon and the Dame stop singing

Dame No, no. There's no top C there, Hubert. It's only a ... (*She sees he is gone*) Hubert? (*Calling uncertainly*) Hubert? Where's he gone?

Ad-lib with the audience, then the singing continues as a duet

The Ghost enters and taps Simon on the shoulder. He stops singing, turns and sees it, screams and exits L, followed by the Ghost

The Dame stops singing and looks around fearfully

Simon? Simon? (*Scared*) Ooo-er. Now he's gone as well. I knew I didn't like this place. (*To the audience*) This is all your fault for not shouting loud enough. Now I'll have to sing on my own. (*She begins to sing again*)

The Ghost enters and taps her on the shoulder

The Dame turns

The Ghost screams and runs off in terror

The Dame turns back to the audience, a disgusted look on her face

Music critics.

As she begins to exit R, the Lights fade quickly to Black-out

SCENE 5

The Giant's Kitchen

A full set. A huge dimensioned kitchen. A great chair is UR. UL is a large chest of jewels, overflowing the sides. On top of this is the King's crown

When the scene begins, armed Guards stand at strategic points overseeing raggedly dressed villagers as they wearily scrub the floor and sing

Song 14 (Prisoners)

At the end of the song, the Giant's voice is heard off L, *and the prisoners cower in fear*

Giant   (*off*) Fee, fi, fo, fum.
                        I smell the blood of Englishmen.
                        Be they alive or be they dead,
                        I'll grind their bones to make my bread.

With much panting and grunting, Blunderbore, the Giant, lumbers on L *and stands glowering at the prisoners. He carries a large club*

Aaaagh. Out of my sight, you miserable maggots, or I'll have you boiled in oil and fed to the dogs. (*Loudly*) Begone.

The prisoners grab their cleaning things and hurriedly exit UR, *followed by the Guards*

Blunderbore lumbers over to his chair and sits

Now bring in my new prisoners. (*He laughs harshly*)

Jack, Princess, King, Dame and Simon are herded in by Rancid who carries both the magic sword and his own. He moves to the Giant and lays the magic sword at the side of the chair before turning to face the prisoners, his own sword at the ready

Simon (*dejectedly*) Hiya, kids.
Dame (*looking at the Giant*) Oooh, it's the Jolly Green Giant. Here, I love your sweetcorn. (*Holding her sides and laughing*) Ho, ho, ho.
Giant (*loudly*) Silence. (*He bangs his club on the table*)
Dame (*to Simon*) Shut up.
Giant Trespassing outside my castle, eh? You're going to suffer for that.
Simon (*groaning*) Oh, no. He's going to sing to us.
King Doesn't bother me. I've heard (*well-known pop singer*).
Giant (*roaring*) Silence.

All react with fright

(*To Rancid*) Take them to the dungeons whilst I decide what to do with them. But leave the girl here. Methinks she's pretty enough to be my bride.
Dame You must be joking. You won't catch me marrying any giant.
Giant Away with them.

Rancid comes forward to escort them off

Jack (*suddenly*) Knock, knock.

Rancid (*turning to him with a snarl*) Who's there?
Jack (*moving closer*) Broker.
Rancid Broker who?
Jack Broker few toes for you. (*He stamps hard on Rancid's foot*)

As Rancid yells with pain, everyone makes a dash for safety

The King, Dame and Simon exit

Rancid manages to grab the Princess by the hand. She screams and Jack attempts to free her without success. The angry Giant gets to his feet with a bellow of rage and moves toward them swinging his club

Princess Run, Jack. Run.

Jack releases her other hand and backs away

Jack (*calling*) Don't worry. I'll be back for you.

Jack exits

Giant (*angrily*) After them, you fool. Call out the Guards.

Rancid releases the Princess and hurries off after Jack

Hurry. Hurry.
Princess (*anxiously*) Oh, please don't hurt them and I'll do anything. Anything at all.
Giant (*snarling*) I'm sure you will, my dear. But die they shall—as all die who dare set foot in this castle. Now come closer and tell me about this miserable country of yours. Serenia, isn't it? I like to know about the places I'm going to destroy. (*He laughs harshly*)
Princess (*bravely*) You'll never destroy Serenia, no matter how hard you try. As soon as Jack comes back, he'll make you wish you'd never *heard* of it.
Giant That pint-sized poppinjay? (*He laughs amusedly*) I'll crush him like a snail beneath my foot. (*He lumbers back to his chair, still chuckling, and sits again*)
Princess (*turning away in despair*) Oh, Jack. I don't know where you are, but please be careful. If anything happens to you, I don't know what I'll do.

Song 15 (Princess)

At the end of the song, Princess hurries off R in tears

The Giant roars with laughter

Giant Now send on tonight's entertainment whilst I wait for my cow pie to arrive.

The Ballet dancers enter and perform a very short classical ballet. They are followed by Simon and the Dame in ballet costumes who perform a Balloon Ballet

Ballet: Dancers. Comic Ballet: Dame and Simon

During this, the Giant falls asleep

At the end of the Ballet, all exit in a flurry

There is a loud snore from the Giant

Jack enters cautiously DR *followed by the King and Princess*

Jack (*softly*) The Giant. He's fallen asleep. Now's our chance. (*He tiptoes to the chair to get his sword*)
Princess (*anxiously*) Be careful.
Giant (*shifting position*) Ahhhhhhhhhh. (*He snores again*)

Jack picks up the sword and backs away

Jack Quick. Run for the beanstalk whilst I deal with him.
King But what about my crown? And all the money he stole?
Jack There it is. (*He indicates the chest*) Do you think you can carry it?
Princess We'll have a good try.

The King and Princess hurry to the chest. The King puts on the crown then they lift the chest and begin to carry it off

Rancid enters R, *sword in hand*

Rancid No sign of them, Master. (*Seeing them*) What?
Jack (*calling*) Run for it.

The King and Princess stagger off with the chest

Rancid hurls himself at Jack. A fierce sword fight takes place. As they battle the Giant begins to wake

Giant (*sleepily*) What's all the noise?
Rancid Help, Master. Help.
Giant (*rousing*) What? What? (*He sits upright*)
Rancid The prisoners. They're escaping.
Giant (*standing with a growl of rage*) Ahhhhhhhh. (*He lifts his club*)
Jack (*to Rancid*) Take that. (*He plunges his sword into Rancid*)

As Rancid falls with a cry, the Giant's club descends, just missing Jack who springs aside

Giant You puny mortal—I'll grind your bones to make my bread.
Jack You'll have to catch me first.

Jack exits DL

Giant (*roaring*) Stop. Come back. Ahhhhhhhh.

The furious Giant lumbers off L in pursuit

The Lights fade rapidly to a Black-out

SCENE 6

On the road back to the beanstalk

A lane scene. Strobe lighting

The Villagers enter L, running, followed by Daisy, the Princess and King (with the chest), the Dame and Simon, and Jack bringing up the rear. All run with exaggerated steps and movements to make the strobe work more effectively. Overlay this with shouts and screams, bass drumbeats for the Giant's footsteps, "chase" music and the Giant's voice shouting: "Stop! Come back!" etc.

Everyone exits R

Black-out. Cut the music and drumbeats

The Fairy enters R, in a white follow spot

Fairy   Down the beanstalk, quickly sliding...
                       'Neath the leaves and flowers hiding.
                       Fleeing feet seek twining stalk;
                       No time to pause, no breath to talk.
                       They race towards the earth below
                       With pounding hearts and cheeks aglow,
                       Whilst close behind, old Blunderbore
                       Pursues them with a fearful roar.
Giant (*off*) Stop. Come back.
Fairy   The halfway mark's in sight at last.
                       They reach it ... and they race on past.
                       No hesitation ... no mistakes...
                       The beanstalk shudders, sways and quakes
                       As Blunderbore increases speed,
                       By now, quite mad at them indeed.
Giant (*off*) Aghhhhhhhhh.
Fairy   Just one more mile to go before
                       They're back outside the Dairy's door,
                       And yet, intent on their undoing
                       Comes the Giant, *still* pursuing.
                       At long, long last they reach the ground

> And from the beanstalk lightly bound,
> So let's rejoin them all once more...
> To see the end of Blunderbore.

She waves her wand and there is an instant black-out

The Fairy exits

Scene 7

Outside the dairy

As Act I, Scene 6. The chest is on the ground DL. *The Villagers, Dame, Simon, King and Princess are clustered around the base of the beanstalk. Jack is just about to drop down from it, sword in hand*

All   (*variously*) Quick. The Giant. He's almost here. (*Etc.*)
Jack   (*jumping down*) Out of the way, everyone.

All rush downstage to the extreme edges

(*Looking upwards*) Right, Mr Giant. See how you like this. (*He swings his sword at the beanstalk*)
Giant   (*off*) No. No. Stop.

Jack strikes again. The beanstalk sways

Nooooooooooooooooo.
Simon   (*looking up*) He's coming down.

All protect their heads and cry out as the stage is plunged into total darkness amidst the sound of great crashing. After a moment, the Lights slowly go up to reveal the beanstalk has gone and everyone is crouched down. They rise and hurry up to the fence and look over it

Dame   Ooooh, I say, what a big hole. He must have gone right through to Australia.
Simon   Serves 'em right for sending us *Neighbours*.

All congratulate each other

Jack   Well that's the end of old Blunderbore. He won't be bothering us any more.
Princess   We've got all our money back.
King   (*happily*) And my crown.
Jack   So everything'll be back to normal in no time.
King   Here, wait a minute, though. (*He looks round*) Where's the old cow?

Dame I'm here, dear.

Simon Not you, Mum. Daisy. (*Worried*) Oh, don't say we've left her up there.

Dame (*beaming*) Course we haven't. I took care of her. I strapped one of my spare balloons onto her and here she comes now.

Daisy enters L, a huge balloon floating from her middle

All laugh delightedly

Jack Well, there's only one thing to do now, and that's claim my reward. (*To the King*) May I marry your daughter, Your Majesty?

Princess Oh, please, Father.

King (*to Jack*) Of course you may. And I'm going to marry your mother.

All congratulate the pairs

The Fairy enters R

Fairy   Brave Jack, now claim your blushing bride.
             You've won your fight. The Giant's died.
             From henceforth bask in joy and laughter,
             And all live happily ever after.

Song 16 (Entire company)

At the end of the song, fast fade to Black-out

SCENE 8

A corridor in the royal palace

A frontcloth scene

Simon enters to do the songsheet routine. The Dame or King may join this at the director's discretion

At the end of the scene, he/they exit

Rapid fade to Black-out

SCENE 9

The royal palace

Full set: a ballroom. Full lighting

FINALE

To a bright melody, the walk-down commences as follows:

Babes
Chorus
Giant (actor holding Giant's head)
Daisy (in character or as actors holding the skin)
Fairy
Rancid
King
Simon
Dame
Jack and Princess

COUPLETS

Jack Our pantomime is over. The final curtain falls.
Princess We hope you've all enjoyed your time within these theatre walls.
Simon So as we wish you all good-night, there's nothing to say but:
Dame If you *have* enjoyed it, tell your friends...
    If not—just keep your mouths shut.

There is a reprise of one of the show's brighter songs and——

—the CURTAIN *falls*

FURNITURE AND PROPERTY LIST

ACT I

SCENE 1

On stage: Cottage and shop front cut-outs

Off stage: Shopping bag (**Dame**)
Whip (**Rancid**)
Almost empty pouch (**Rancid**)
Bucket and stool (**Simon**)

Personal: **Fairy:** wand (used throughout)
King: crown
Daisy: tin of milk

SCENE 2

On stage: Nil

Personal: **Daisy:** tether

SCENE 3

On stage: Tents
Stalls
Cattle-pens
Trees

Personal: **Gypsies:** tambourines
Citizens: purses
King: tatty-looking crown
Rancid: whip, 2 small, well-filled bags: one containing gold, one containing
beans

SCENE 4

On stage: Nil

Off stage: Small bag full of beans (**Jack**)

SCENE 5

On stage: Dressing as required

Off stage: Small bag full of beans (**Jack**)

SCENE 6

On stage: Picket fence
Beanstalk

Off stage: Stuffed toy (**Simon**)

ACT II

SCENE 1

On stage: Trees

SCENE 2

On stage: Nil

Off stage: Sword (**Fairy**)

SCENE 3

On stage: Gigantic Venus fly-trap and other evil-looking plants

Off stage: Sword (**Jack**)

Personal: **Rancid:** sword

SCENE 4

On stage: Nil

Off stage: Swords (**Guards**)
Sword (**Rancid**)

Personal: **Jack:** sword

SCENE 5

On stage: Huge chair UR
Large table
Large chest overflowing with jewels. *On top:* **King**'s crown
Scrubbing brushes, buckets, etc.

Off stage: Large club (**Giant**)
2 swords (**Rancid**)

Personal: **Guards:** swords

SCENE 6

On stage: Nil

Off stage: Chest of jewels (**King** and **Princess**)

SCENE 7

On stage: Picket fence
Beanstalk
Sword (for **Jack**)

During black-out on page 44:

Strike: Beanstalk

Personal: **Daisy:** huge balloon

SCENE 8

On stage: Songsheet

SCENE 9

On stage: Nil

LIGHTING PLOT

Property fittings required: nil

Various interior and exterior settings

ACT I, Scene 1 (Full stage)

To open: Full, general lighting

Cue 1	Everyone exits at the end of Song 2 *Dim lighting*	(Page 3)
Cue 2	**Rancid** laughs harshly and exits L *Revert to full general lighting*	(Page 4)
Cue 3	**Daisy** hangs her head in sorrow *Slow fade to black-out*	(Page 13)

ACT I, Scene 2 (Frontcloth)

To open: General lighting downstage

Cue 4	Everyone exits R at the end of Song 4 *Fade to black-out*	(Page 15)

ACT I, Scene 3 (Full stage)

To open: Full, general lighting

Cue 5	**Rancid** drags off the **Princess** and **Daisy** *Quick fade to black-out*	(Page 20)

ACT I, Scene 4 (Frontcloth)

Cue 6	**Jack** and **Simon** exit at the end of Song 6 *Quick fade to black-out*	(Page 21)

ACT I, Scene 5 (Full or three-quarter stage)

To open: Full, general interior lighting; evening effect through window, gradually darkening

Cue 7	**Jack** exits *Fade to black-out. When ready, bring up follow spot on* **Fairy***; fade as she exits*	(Page 24)

ACT I, Scene 6 (Full stage)

To open: Full, general lighting

No cues

ACT II, SCENE 1 (Full stage)

To open: Full, general lighting

Cue 8	**Fairy Thistledown** waves her wand	(Page 28)
	Quick fade to black-out. When ready bring up UV lighting	
Cue 9	The **Butterflies**, etc., exit	(Page 28)
	Snap off UV lighting and bring up follow spot on **Fairy**	
Cue 10	The **Fairy** exits at the end of the song	(Page 28)
	Snap off follow spot and bring up full, general lighting	
Cue 11	Everyone exits in all directions	(Page 30)
	Quick fade to black-out	

ACT II, SCENE 2 (Frontcloth)

To open: General lighting downstage

Cue 12	**Jack** exits L	(Page 31)
	Quick fade to black-out	

ACT II, SCENE 3 (Full stage)

To open: Full, general lighting

Cue 13	The **King** and **Dame** exit	(Page 35)
	Quick fade to black-out	

ACT II, SCENE 4 (Frontcloth)

To open: Dim green/blue lighting downstage

Cue 14	The **Dame** begins to exit	(Page 39)
	Quick fade to black-out	

ACT II, SCENE 5 (Full stage)

To open: Full, general lighting

Cue 15	The furious **Giant** lumbers off L in pursuit	(Page 43)
	Quick fade to black-out	

ACT II, SCENE 6 (Frontcloth)

To open: Strobe lighting

Cue 16	All exit R	(Page 43)
	Black-out; bring up white follow spot on **Fairy**	
Cue 17	The **Fairy** waves her wand	(Page 44)
	Black-out	

ACT II, SCENE 7 (Full stage)

To open: Full, general lighting

Cue 18	**Simon:** "He's coming down."	(Page 44)
	Black-out; when ready, bring up full, general lighting	
Cue 19	At the end of Song 16	(Page 45)
	Quick fade to black-out	

ACT II, SCENE 8 (Frontcloth)

To open: General lighting downstage

Cue 20   At the end of the songsheet routine   (Page 45)
             Quick fade to black-out

ACT II, SCENE 9 (Full stage)

To open: Full, general lighting

No cues

EFFECTS PLOT

ACT I

Cue 1	**Simple Simon** exits DR *Fanfare*	(Page 5)
Cue 2	To open SCENE 6 *Mist around beanstalk base*	(Page 25)

ACT II

Cue 3	To open SCENE 6 *Shouts, screams, bass drumbeats, "chase" music, **Giant***'s voice*	(Page 43)
Cue 4	Everyone exits R *Cut all effects*	(Page 43)
Cue 5	**Simon:** "He's coming down." *Great crashing sound*	(Page 44)

Printed by Black Bear Press Limited, Cambridge, England